VITALITY ON YOUR PLATE

VITALITY ON YOUR PLATE

33 LIVING FOOD RECIPES FOR EFFORTLESS WELLNESS

Dr. Kris Harm BSc DC LCC

Copyright © 2023 by Dr. Kris Harm BSc DC LCC

All rights reserved.

No part of this publication may be reproduced, distributed, or transmitted in any form or by any means, including photocopying, recording, or other electronic or mechanical methods, without the prior written permission of the publisher, except as permitted by copyright law. Brief quotations embedded in articles or reviews are exempt.

First edition 2023

Table of Contents

Welcome 8

Chapter 1: Breakfast Boosts 10

    1. Green Power Smoothie Bowl 10

    2. Veggie-Packed Omelette 12

    3. Overnight Chia Seed Pudding 14

    4. Superfood Breakfast Bowl 16

    5. Hearty Quinoa Breakfast Bowl 18

    6. Mediterranean Breakfast Wrap 20

Chapter 2: Fresh Starters 22

    7. Mediterranean Quinoa Salad 22

    8. Avocado Stuffed with Chickpea Salad 24

    9. Caprese Stuffed Portobello Mushrooms 26

    10. Zucchini and Carrot Fritters 28

    11. Spinach and Feta Stuffed Mushrooms 30

    12. Cucumber Bites with Tuna Salad 32

    13. Stuffed Bell Pepper Boats 34

    14. Greek Yogurt and Herb Dip with Veggie Sticks 36

Chapter 3: Wholesome Bowls 38

    15. Teriyaki Tofu Stir-Fry 38

    16. Lentil and Quinoa Bowl 42

    17. Quinoa and Black Bean Burrito Bowl 44

18. Mediterranean Chickpea and Quinoa Bowl 46

19. Sweet Potato and Black Bean Buddha Bowl 48

Chapter 4: Speedy Suppers 50

20. Lemon Garlic Tofu with Zoodles...50

21. Chickpea Pasta Aglio e Olio with Broccoli 52

22. Teriyaki Vegetable Stir-Fry with Rice 54

23. Mediterranean Chickpea Salad Wraps 56

24. Sheet Pan Lemon Herb Salmon and Vegetables 58

Chapter 5: Smart Sides 60

25. Roasted Brussels Sprouts with Tahini Dressing 60

26. Broccoli Rice Pilaf..62

27. Grilled Asparagus and Quinoa Salad 64

28. Spinach and Mushroom Quinoa Stuffed Bell Peppers 66

Chapter 6: Guilt-free Treats 68

29. Dark Chocolate and Berry Parfait...68

30. Nut Butter Banana Bites 70

31. Almond Butter Energy Bites 72

32. Greek Yogurt Parfait with Mixed Nuts and Honey 74

33. Chocolate Dipped Strawberries 76

Conclusion 78

Welcome

In a world where time is precious and well-being is paramount, I invite you to join me on a culinary journey that embraces convenience without compromising on health or taste. I welcome you to this cookbook because I believe that nourishing your body should never be a daunting task.

Life's demands can be relentless, leaving little room for preparing nutritious meals. My cookbook is your solution – 33 recipes meticulously crafted to infuse your days with vitality and flavour, all achievable in just 30 minutes. I have carefully curated dishes that celebrate clean proteins, vibrant vegetables, and the beauty of simplicity.

Radiate health with each bite as you explore the collection of dishes that honour the harmony between taste and well-being. The recipes not only provide essential nutrients but also incorporate a glorious array of colours and textures to tantalise the senses and elevate your dining experience.

Whether you're a busy professional, a dedicated parent, or anyone seeking a journey towards wholesome living, this cookbook will guide you on a culinary adventure that bridges the gap between time constraints and good health.

Within these pages, you'll find creative recipes that transcend traditional notions of healthy eating, proving that nourishment can be swift, delightful, and truly satisfying.

A Fusion of Flavours, A Fusion of Lifestyles – there are many diverse dietary preferences that shape our lives. Hence, for every recipe, I offer vegetarian alternatives, allowing you to seamlessly transition from meat to plant-based options without compromising on taste or nutrition. Flexibility, after all, is key to achieving your wellness goals.

My welcome to you extends beyond the pages of this cookbook. It's an invitation to not just cook, but to craft nourishment, to empower your well-being and to relish every moment spent in the kitchen. The recipes herein not only celebrate nutritious ingredients but also celebrate you – your journey towards a healthier you, your pursuit of balance, and your desire to shine.

Let's ignite the spark of well-being together – one delightful, wholesome meal at a time.

Let's live life to the fullest and

Stay Radiant, Stay Nourished, Stay Vibrant!

Chapter 1: Breakfast Boosts

1. Green Power Smoothie Bowl

Time required to Prepare it: 10 mins

Time required to Cook it: 0 mins

Portions: 1

Ingredients:

- 1 cup of leafy greens
- Half cup of water or plant-based milk
- 1 tbsp chia seeds
- Half cup of Greek yogurt (or choose vegan yogurt for a plant-based option)
- Half cup of assorted berries

Optional toppings: sliced fruits, nuts, seeds, coconut flakes

Method:

- Leafy greens, various berries, Greek yogurt, chia seeds, & water/plant-based milk should all be blended.
- Blend until creamy and smooth, adding more liquid if necessary.
- Put smoothie in a bowl, please.
- Sprinkle with shredded coconut, diced fruits, nuts, seeds, or nut butter.

Calories: 250

Nutrition: Packed with vitamins, minerals, antioxidants, and protein.

2. Veggie-Packed Omelette

Time required to Prepare it: 10 mins

Time required to Cook it: 10 mins

Portions: 1

Ingredients:

- Cooking spray
- Pepper and salt to adjust the taste
- 1/4 cup of diced bell peppers (a mix of different colors)
- 3 egg whites
- 1/4 cup spinach
- 2 tbsp of crumbled feta cheese (or use nutritional yeast for a dairy-free option)

Method:

- Egg whites should be beaten until they reach the "stiff peaks" stage.
- Preheat a nonstick pan over medium heat with a small amount of cooking spray or olive oil.
- Whisk the egg whites and then add them to the pan.
- Onto one side of the omelette, evenly distribute the chopped bell peppers, minced spinach, & scattered feta cheese (or nutritious yeast).
- Sprinkle some Pepper and salt on it.
- When the omelet's edges are firm and the bottom gets lightly browned, carefully fold the uncooked side over the cooked side.
- Wait two or three mins more for a firm omelette in the center.

Calories: 200-250

Nutrition: High protein and fiber content, packed with vitamins and minerals.

3. Overnight Chia Seed Pudding

Time required to Prepare it: 5 mins

Time required to Cook it: 0 mins (overnight setting time required)

Portions: 1

Ingredients:

- 1/2 cup of assorted fresh fruits (such as berries, mango, banana)
- 1/4 cup of chia seeds
- 1 tbsp of honey or you can use maple syrup, Nuts or seeds for topping (All these is optional)
- 1 cup of plant-based milk (like almond milk)

Method:

- Put the chia seeds & almond milk into a sealed container and shake well. needs a vigorous stirring to combine.
- Wait a few mins for the mixture to settle to prevent clumping.
- Cover and chill for at least four to six hrs, preferably overnight.
- Give it a thorough swirl before serving.
- Fresh fruits, honey/maple syrup, and nuts/seeds are optional toppings.

Calories: 250-300

Nutrition: High in fiber, healthy fats, and antioxidants.

4. Superfood Breakfast Bowl

Time required to Prepare it: 10 mins

Time required to Cook it: 0 mins

Portions: 1

Ingredients:

- Half cup of mixed berries
- Half cup of cooked oats or quinoa
- 1 small banana
- 1/2 cup Greek yogurt (or a plant-based vegan yogurt)
- 1 tbsp of almond butter or your preferred nut/seed butter
- Handful of spinach or kale leaves
- 1 tbsp of chia seeds

Optional toppings: chopped nuts, seeds, honey or maple syrup

Method:

- Prepared quinoa or oats can be used as a base by layering them in a dish.
- Greek yogurt, sliced bananas, mixed berries, chia seeds, & almond butter on top.
- For a healthy dose of greens, throw in some spinach or kale.
- Finish with optional toppings like chopped nuts, seeds, and a drizzle of honey or maple syrup.
- Mix everything together before enjoying.

Calories: 300

Nutrition: High in protein, fiber, antioxidants, and essential nutrients.

5. Hearty Quinoa Breakfast Bowl

Time required to Prepare it: 10 mins

Time required to Cook it: 15 mins

Portions: 2

Ingredients:

- 1 cup of quinoa, drained and thoroughly rinsed
- 1 cup of assorted mixed vegetables (such as spinach, cherry tomatoes, bell peppers)
- Pepper and salt to adjust the flavor
- 4 eggs (or use tofu scramble as a vegetarian alternative)
- 2 cups of vegetable broth or water
- Fresh herbs
- 1/2 cup of cooked black beans or chickpeas
- 1 tbsp of olive oil

Method:

- Bring a pot of water as well as vegetable broth to a boil and add the quinoa.
- Quinoa is done when it is mushy and every drop of water has been absorbed, which takes around 15 mins when simmered covered over low heat.
- Use a fork to fluff the ingredients.
- Olive oil should be melted using a separate pan over low to medium heat. The vegetable mixture needs a few mins in a sauté pan to soften.
- Crack the eggs into the space left when the vegetables are pushed to the opposite side of the pan. Mix the scrambled eggs with the vegetables that have been sautéed.
- Sprinkle some prepared black beans or as chickpeas over the quinoa and then pile on the egg and vegetable mixture.
- Add some Pepper and salt and some fresh herbs for presentation.
- Quickly dish up a bowl of the wholesome quinoa breakfast.

Calories: 350

Nutrition: Packed with protein, fiber, and essential nutrients.

6. Mediterranean Breakfast Wrap

Time required to Prepare it: 15 mins

Time required to Cook it: 5 mins

Portions: 2 servings

Ingredients:

- 1/4 cup cucumbers
- 1/4 cup spinach
- 2 eggs (or tofu scramble for a vegetarian alternative)
- Pepper and salt to adjust the taste
- 2 tbsp herbs
- Half cup tomatoes
- 2 whole wheat tortillas (or opt for gluten-free tortillas)
- 1/4 cup feta cheese (or opt for nutritional yeast as a dairy-free alternative)

Optional: hot sauce or salsa for extra flavor

Method:

- Beat the eggs in a bowl. Add pepper and salt to taste.
- To achieve the desired doneness in eggs, fry them over medium heat in a pan that won't stick. The same method works for making tofu scramble.
- Lay out the tortillas and divide the scrambled eggs (or tofu) between them.
- Top with chopped spinach, diced tomatoes, diced cucumbers, and crumbled feta cheese (or nutritional yeast).
- Additional fresh herbs, salt, & pepper, to taste.
- Make wraps out of the tortillas.
- Serve the Mediterranean breakfast wraps with a side of hot sauce or salsa if desired.

Calories: 300

Nutrition: Provides a balanced mix of protein, fiber, and vitamins.

Chapter 2: Fresh Starters

7. Mediterranean Quinoa Salad

Time required to Prepare it: 15 mins

Time required to Cook it: 15 mins

Portions: 2

Ingredients:

- 3 tbsp olive oil
- 1 cup of quinoa, drained and thoroughly rinsed
- 1 cup cherry tomatoes
- 1/2 cup of sliced Kalamata olives, pitted

- 1 cucumber, diced
- 1/4 cup parsley
- Pepper and salt to suit your taste
- Half cup of feta cheese, crumbled (or use tofu cubes for a vegetarian choice)
- Juice of 1 lemon
- 2 cups of water

Method:

- The quinoa and water should be brought to a boil in a medium saucepan. For 15 mins on low heat, covered, the quinoa will absorb the water and be ready to eat.
- After it has cooled for a time, use a fork to fluff it.
- Mix the quinoa, tomatoes, cucumbers, olives, feta (or rather, tofu) pieces, and chopped parsley in a large bowl.
- Vinaigrette is made by combining the olive oil, the juice from a single lemon, powdered black pepper, & salt in a small basin.
- Toss the quinoa mixture with the vinaigrette to coat.
- Try it out, and season it to your liking.
- You can either eat the salad right immediately, or put it in the fridge to enjoy at a later time.

Calories: 350

Nutrition: Protein, fiber, and good fats abound.

8. Avocado Stuffed with Chickpea Salad

Time required to Prepare it: 15 mins

Time required to Cook it: 0 mins

Portions: 2

Ingredients:

- 1/4 cup chopped red onion
- 1 tbsp olive oil
- 2 ripe avocados, halved and pitted
- 1/4 cup chopped cilantro
- Juice of 1 lime
- Pepper and salt to taste
- 1 can (15 oz) chickpeas

Optional: diced zucchini and bell peppers

Method:

- The chickpeas can be roughly mashed using a fork as well as a potato masher.
- To the mashed chickpeas, incorporate the red onions, cilantro, juice of one lime, salt, pepper, and olive oil. Toss everything together.
- Diced zucchini & bell peppers, if using, should be added to the chickpea mix at this point.
- Each avocado half should have a little well carved out of the flesh.
- Fill the cavities of the avocado halves with the chickpea salad mixture.
- Serve the stuffed avocados immediately.

Calories: 350

Nutrition: Contains a lot of fiber, good fats, and protein from plants.

9. Caprese Stuffed Portobello Mushrooms

Time required to Prepare it: 10 mins

Time required to Cook it: 15 mins

Portions: 4

Ingredients:

- 4 large portobello mushrooms, stems carefully removed
- 2 tbsp olive oil
- 2 tbsp of balsamic vinegar
- Pepper and salt to taste
- 1/4 cup basil leaves
- 1/4 cup diced mozzarella cheese

- 1 cup halved cherry tomatoes

Method:

- Preheating the oven to 375°F (190 degrees Celsius) is suggested.
- Cherry tomatoes, vegan mozzarella, fresh basil, balsamic vinegar, & some Pepper and salt should be combined in a bowl and mixed thoroughly.
- Arrange the portobello mushrooms, gill sides up, on a baking sheet.
- Fill the mushrooms halfway with the tomato-mozzarella mixture.
- For approximately 15 mins in an oven preheated to 350 degrees, up to the point the mushrooms are soft and the cheese is warmed.
- Serve the Caprese stuffed portobello mushrooms warm.

Calories: 150-180

Nutrition: Rich in protein, antioxidants, and essential nutrients.

10. Zucchini and Carrot Fritters

Time required to Prepare it: 15 mins

Time required to Cook it: 10 mins

Portions: 4

Ingredients:

- 1/4 cup of chopped fresh herbs
- 2 medium carrots, grated
- 2 medium zucchinis
- Pepper and salt to adjust the flavor
- 2 eggs (or utilize flax eggs for a vegan choice)
- Half cup whole wheat flour (or opt for chickpea flour for gluten-free)
- 1/4 cup of minced fresh garlic

- Olive oil for the frying process

Method:

- Mix the garlic, flour, salt, carrots, shredded zucchini, egg yolks, herbs, and pepper together in a large basin. Throw everything together.
- Start by heating some olive oil inside a pan over moderate heat.
- Using a spoon, portion out the zucchini-carrot mixture, and flatten it into fritters on a skillet.
- Make sure the fritters are cooked through by frying them for three to four minutes on each side.
- Place the finished fritters on a platter lined folded paper towels to soak up any remaining oil.
- Warm the fritters and serve with a yogurt-based dipping sauce as well as salsa on the side.

Calories: 120-150

Nutrition: Packed with fiber, vitamins, and minerals.

11. Spinach and Feta Stuffed Mushrooms

Time required to Prepare it: 10 mins

Time required to Cook it: 15 mins

Portions: 4

Ingredients:

- 1/2 cup feta cheese (or choose vegan feta)
- 2 cloves garlic
- 1 tbsp of olive oil
- 12 large button mushrooms, carefully remove and finely chop the stems
- Pepper and salt to suit your taste
- 1/4 cup of grated Parmesan cheese (or select nutritional yeast for a dairy-free alternative)

- 2 cups of chopped baby spinach

Method:

- It is suggested that oven temperature be set to 375 F (190 C).
- Olive oil in a skillet over an ambient to medium temperature is ideal.
- Mince the mushroom stems and combine them with the garlic. You should let the mushrooms drain for a few mins before serving.
- Cook the baby spinach until it wilts after being added to the pan.
- Mix in the crumbled feta (or vegan feta) & grated Parmesan (or nutritional yeast) after taking the skillet off the heat. Sprinkle some Pepper and salt on it.
- Fill the voids in the mushrooms with the spinach and feta.
- Bake the stuffed mushrooms for 15 minutes at 400 degrees Fahrenheit, or until the filling is bubbling.
- Warm the mushrooms that have been packed with spinach and feta.

Calories: 100-130

Nutrition: Provides protein, fiber, and a variety of nutrients.

12. Cucumber Bites with Tuna Salad

Time required to Prepare it: 15 mins

Time required to Cook it: 0 mins

Portions: 12 cucumber bites

Ingredients:

- Pepper and salt as per your preference
- 1 large cucumber
- 1 tsp lemon juice
- 1/4 cup diced celery
- 1 can (5 oz) tuna, drained
- Chopped dill or parsley for garnish
- 2 tbsp finely chopped red onion
- 2 tbsp Greek yogurt

Method:

- After you've washed the cucumber well, cut it into 1-inch chunks.
- Carefully scoop out the pulp from the center of every cucumber slice using a baller for melon or a small spoon.
- Get your ducks in a row before you take off.
- Tuna should be drained before being combined with the other ingredients in a bowl.
- Mound the tuna salad mixture gently in each cucumber cup and serve.
- Sliced fresh dill and parsley adds a burst of flavor and brightness as a garnish.
- Serve the cucumber bites at once by arranging them in a pretty pattern on a serving plate.

Calories: 25 calories

Nutrition: Packed with protein, vitamin K and potassium.

13. Stuffed Bell Pepper Boats

Time required to Prepare it: 15 mins

Time required to Cook it: 15 mins

Portions: 4 servings

Ingredients:

- 1/4 cup of black beans
- Half cup of cooked quinoa
- 1/4 cup of corn kernels
- Pepper and salt to suit your taste
- 2 large bell peppers
- Half cup of lean ground turkey or chicken
- 1/4 cup diced tomatoes
- 1 tsp of taco seasoning

Method:

- Preheating the oven to 375°F (190 degrees Celsius) is suggested.
- Peppers should be halved lengthwise and the membranes & seeds removed.
- Lean ground turkey or as chicken should be cooked in a skillet until it loses its pink color. Mix in some taco spice, corn, black beans, sliced tomatoes, and corn. Add two more mins of cooking time.
- Mix the cooked quinoa in thoroughly.
- Lightly pack the turkey or chicken mixture into each bell pepper half.
- Bake your stuffed pepper halves in a preheated oven for 15 mins, up to the point the peppers are tender.
- Serve the stuffed bell pepper boats warm.

Calories: 130 calories

Nutrition: Packed with proteins, vitamin A and C.

14. Greek Yogurt and Herb Dip with Veggie Sticks

Time required to Prepare it: 10 mins

Time required to Cook it: 0 mins

Portions: Serves 4

Ingredients:

- 2 tbsp of herbs
- Assorted vegetable sticks (carrots, cucumbers, bell peppers) for dipping
- 1 tsp of minced garlic
- 1 cup of Greek yogurt
- Pepper and salt to adjust the taste
- 1 tsp of lemon juice

Method:

- Greek yogurt, fresh herbs, garlic, the juice of one lemon, salt, & pepper should all be mixed together in a basin. Combine thoroughly by mixing for a few mins.
- Try it out, and if it needs more salt, add it.
- The vegetables should be washed, peeled, and cut into sticks.
- Greek yogurt with herbs can be served as a dip with vegetable sticks.

Calories: 45 calories

Nutrition: Packed with vitamins and minerals.

Chapter 3: Wholesome Bowls

15. Teriyaki Tofu Stir-Fry

Time required to Prepare it: 15 mins

Time required to Cook it: 15 mins

Portions: 2

Ingredients:

- 1 block (14 oz) firm tofu, pressed and cubed (or tempeh/seitan)
- 2 cloves garlic

- 1 tbsp of honey or maple syrup
- 1 cup colorful bell peppers, sliced
- 1 tbsp of vegetable oil
- 1 tsp of sesame oil
- 1 cup of snap peas or snow peas, trimmed
- 1 tsp of grated fresh ginger
- 2 tbsp of low-sodium soy sauce
- 1 tsp of cornstarch
- 1 cup of broccoli florets
- 2 tbsp of water

Optional toppings: sesame seeds, green onions

Method:

- Whisk together the soy sauce, water, honey or maple syrup, corn starch, oil of sesame seeds, chopped ginger, and minced garlic to make the teriyaki sauce. Set aside.
- Vegetable oil should be heated over a medium to low flame in a large skillet or wok.
- To make some crispy, golden tofu cubes, simply fry them in oil. Take out of the frying pan.
- Bell peppers, broccoli, & snap peas can be stir-fried in the same pan with a little extra oil if necessary until they are cooked but still retain their crunch for a few mins.
- Back in the pan, top the fried tofu with a drizzle of teriyaki sauce.

- Stir the tofu and vegetables around in the sauce until everything is well-coated and the sauce has thickened.
- Sprinkle some sesame seeds and green onions over hot noodles or rice and top with the stir-fry.

Calories: 300-350

Nutrition: There is a plethora of useful nutrients, including protein, fiber, and other vitamins and minerals.

16. Lentil and Quinoa Bowl

Time required to Prepare it: 10 mins

Time required to Cook it: 20 mins

Portions: 2

Ingredients:

- 1 cup cooked quinoa
- 2 cups spinach
- Pepper and salt as per your preference
- 1 tbsp olive oil
- 1 cup cooked lentils
- 1 large sweet potato

Optional: lemon juice, chopped fresh herbs

Method:

- To bake well, an oven temperature of 400°F (200 degrees Celsius) should be set.

- Olive oil, salt, and pepper should be mixed into cubed sweet potatoes.
- Cook the sweet potatoes till they're fork-tender but still have a slight crunch by roasting them in just one layer on a baking pan. It should take about 20 minutes to do this.
- Fresh spinach should be sautéed in a big skillet until it wilts.
- Prepared quinoa, lentils, browned sweet potatoes, & sautéed spinach are assembled in a bowl and served to the table.
- Salt, pepper, and lemon juice can be added to taste.
- If fresh herbs are available, sprinkle them on top.

Calories: 350-400 (varies based on ingredients and portion sizes)

Nutrition: High in protein, fiber, and a variety of nutrients.

17. Quinoa and Black Bean Burrito Bowl

Time required to Prepare it: 10 mins

Time required to Cook it: 15 mins

Portions: 2

Ingredients:

- 1 tsp chili powder
- Pepper and salt to adjust the taste
- 1 cup diced bell peppers
- 1 cup corn kernels
- 1 cup cooked quinoa
- 1 avocado, sliced
- Juice of 1 lime

- 1/2 cup diced red onion
- 1/4 cup cilantro
- 1 can (15 oz) black beans

Optional toppings: Greek yogurt or dairy-free yogurt, salsa, shredded cheese (vegan or regular)

Method:

- Scoop out the black beans from the can and add them to the bowl with the diced bell pepper and red onion.
- Separately from the remainder of the ingredients, combine the pepper, lime juice, salt, chili powder, into a small bowl.
- Mix the dressing into the quinoa so that it is evenly distributed.
- Make sure each person has their own bowl of quinoa.
- Sprinkle with your preferred amount of sliced avocado, minced cilantro, and other toppings.
- Serve the quinoa and black bean burrito bowls immediately.

Calories: 350-400

Nutrition: High in protein, fiber, and essential nutrients.

18. Mediterranean Chickpea and Quinoa Bowl

Time required to Prepare it: 15 mins

Time required to Cook it: 15 mins

Portions: 2

Ingredients:

- Juice of 1 lemon
- 1/4 cup red onion
- 1/4 cup Kalamata olives
- 1 can (15 oz) of drained and rinsed chickpeas
- 2 tsps of dried oregano
- 1 cup of cooked quinoa
- 1/4 cup of diced cucumber

- Pepper and salt to adjust the taste
- 1 cup cherry tomatoes
- Parsley for garnish
- 2 tbsp olive oil
- 1/4 cup feta cheese (or opt for vegan feta)

Method:

- Mix the quinoa, chickpeas, tomatoes, cucumber, onion, olives, and feta (or vegan feta) in a bowl.
- Dressing can be made by combining the juice of one lemon, olive oil, zest of one lemon, dry oregano, salt, and pepper in a small bowl and whisking until smooth.
- Toss the quinoa & chickpeas to combine after dumping the dressing over the top.
- Separate the quinoa and chickpea mixture for the Mediterranean into separate dishes.
- Sprinkle with chopped fresh parsley.
- Quickly dish up a bowl of the Mediterranean quinoa and chickpea salad.

Calories: 350

Nutrition: Provides a combination of plant-based protein, fiber, and essential nutrients.

19. Sweet Potato and Black Bean Buddha Bowl

Time required to Prepare it: 10 mins

Time required to Cook it: 20 mins

Portions: 2

Ingredients:

- Pepper and salt to adjust the taste
- 1 tbsp of tahini dressing
- 1 tsp of smoked paprika
- 1 can (15 oz) of black beans
- 1 tbsp olive oil
- 2 medium sweet potatoes
- 1/4 cup pumpkin seeds or sunflower seeds
- 2 cups spinach

- 1 avocado, sliced

Method:

- Make sure your oven is preheated at 400 degrees Fahrenheit (200 degrees Celsius).
- Cube some sweet potatoes and mix them with olive oil with some salt, pepper, & smoked paprika. To make them tender and somewhat crisp, roast them at 400 degrees for 20 mins.
- Mix some salt into the black beans in a bowl.
- Assemble the bowls by dividing the baby spinach or mixed greens between them.
- Top with roasted sweet potatoes, seasoned black beans, sliced avocado, and pumpkin seeds or sunflower seeds.
- Drizzle tahini dressing over each bowl.
- Serve the sweet potato and black bean Buddha bowls immediately.

Calories: 300

Nutrition: Rich in plant-based protein, fiber, healthy fats, and vitamins.

Chapter 4: Speedy Suppers

20. Lemon Garlic Tofu with Zoodles

Time required to Prepare it: 15 mins

Time required to Cook it: 10 mins

Portions: 2

Ingredients:

- 1 block (14 oz) firm tofu
- Pepper and salt to suit your taste
- 2-3 medium zucchinis, spiralized into zoodles
- 3 cloves of minced garlic
- Zest and juice of 1 lemon
- 2 tbsp of olive oil

- Parsley for garnish

Method:

- In a pan, heat the olive oil above a medium-high flame.
- Brown the tofu pieces on all sides in a skillet. Remove from the heat.
- The remaining olive oil as well as the garlic should be added to the same pan. Let them sizzle for a few seconds to bring out their flavor.
- Sauté the zoodles (noodles made from zucchini) for 2–3 mins, or until they are just soft.
- Pepper and salt should be added after the zest and juice of the lemon have been incorporated.
- Put the cooked tofu back in the pan and stir it all up.
- Garnish the zoodles with chopped parsley and top with the lemon garlic tofu.

Calories: 300

Nutrition: Rich in protein, fiber, and vitamins.

21. Chickpea Pasta Aglio e Olio with Broccoli

Time required to Prepare it: 10 mins

Time required to Cook it: 15 mins

Portions: 2

Ingredients:

- 6 oz chickpea or lentil pasta (or whole wheat spaghetti)
- 3 cloves of thinly sliced garlic
- 3 tbsp of olive oil
- Salt to taste
- 2 cups broccoli florets
- 1/2 tsp of red pepper flakes
- 3 cloves of thinly sliced garlic

Optional: grated Parmesan cheese (or nutritional yeast for a vegan option)

Method:

- Pasta should be prepared in accordance with the directions on the box. Drain and put away.
- Olive oil ought to be warmed in a big skillet over moderate to low heat.
- To amp up the flavor, add some cloves of garlic & crushed red pepper.
- To get a garlic flavor without browning it, sauté it for a minute.
- The florets of broccoli should be added to the pan and sautéed for about 5 mins, or until they reach the desired texture of tender crispiness.
- Toss the cooked pasta into the skillet with the rest of the ingredients.
- To taste, add salt.
- Sprinkle grated Parmesan cheese as well as nutritional yeast on top of the spaghetti aglio e olio before serving if you like.

Calories: 350

Nutrition: High in protein, fiber, and essential nutrients.

22. Teriyaki Vegetable Stir-Fry with Rice

Time required to Prepare it: 10 mins

Time required to Cook it: 15 mins

Portions: 2

Ingredients:

- 1/4 cup of low-sodium teriyaki sauce
- 1 cup of cooked brown rice
- 2 tbsp of olive oil
- Chopped green onions for garnish
- 1 tbsp of sesame seeds (optional)
- 2 cups of mixed vegetables

Method:

- In a big skillet or wok, melt the olive oil over medium heat.
- After about 5-7 mins of stirring, the mixed veggies should be soft but still slightly crisp.
- Toss the vegetables in the teriyaki sauce to ensure they are uniformly coated.
- Put some brown rice in bowls for everyone.
- The teriyaki stir-fry vegetables should be served on the rice.
- Sprinkle with toasted sesame seeds and green onion tops.
- The teriyaki stir-fry vegetables should be served immediately with hot rice.

Calories: 300-350 (varies based on ingredients and portion sizes)

Nutrition: Provides a balance of carbohydrates, vegetables, and flavor.

23. Mediterranean Chickpea Salad Wraps

Time required to Prepare it: 15 mins

Time required to Cook it: 0 mins

Portions: 2

Ingredients:

- 1 cup diced cucumber
- 1/4 cup parsley
- 1/4 cup diced red onion
- 2 tbsp olive oil
- 1 cup diced tomatoes
- Juice of 1 lemon
- Pepper and salt to taste

- 2 whole wheat tortillas (or opt for gluten-free tortillas if desired)
- 1 can (15 oz) chickpeas

Optional: crumbled feta cheese (or vegan feta)

Method:

- Chickpeas, cucumber, tomatoes, red onion, & chopped parsley should all be mixed together in a basin.
- Dressing can be made by combining the pulp of one lemon with the oil from the olives, pepper, & salt in a tiny container and whisking until smooth.
- Toss the chickpeas with the dressing to coat.
- Lay out the tortillas and divide the Mediterranean chickpea salad between them.
- If using, sprinkle crumbled feta cheese over the salad.
- Roll up the tortillas into wraps.
- Serve the Mediterranean chickpea salad wraps immediately.

Calories: 300-350 (varies based on ingredients and portion sizes)

Nutrition: fiber, protein, and a wide range of plant-based tastes.

24. Sheet Pan Lemon Herb Salmon and Vegetables

Time required to Prepare it: 10 mins

Time required to Cook it: 20 mins

Portions: 2

Ingredients:

- Pepper and salt to adjust the taste
- 2 cloves garlic
- Lemon slices for garnish
- Juice of 1 lemon
- 2 tbsp of olive oil
- 1 tsp of dried herbs
- 2 salmon fillets
- 2 cups of mixed vegetables

Method:

- Get your oven ready by heating it to a temperature of at least 400F (200C).
- Salmon fillets and assorted vegetables should be spread out on a baking sheet.
- Salt, garlic, spices, and pepper should be mixed with the juice of one lemon, olive oil, & lemon zest in a small bowl.
- Make sure the salmon and vegetables are evenly covered by tossing them in the olive oil mixture.
- Lemon slices should be arranged on the salmon fillets.
- The salmon is done when it is opaque all of the way and it flakes easily when checked, usually after 15 to 20 mins inside a preheated oven.
- The salmon with the lemon herb sauce and the veggies can be served right away.

Calories: 350-400

Nutrition: Protein, healthy fats, and other nutrients such as omega-3s can all be found in plenty.

Chapter 5: Smart Sides

25. Roasted Brussels Sprouts with Tahini Dressing

Time required to Prepare it: 10 mins

Time required to Cook it: 20 mins

Portions: 2

Ingredients:

- 2 tbsp tahini
- 1 clove minced garlic
- Pepper and salt to taste
- 2 tbsp olive oil

- 2 tbsp lemon juice
- Water (to thin the dressing, as needed)
- 1 lb Brussels sprouts, halved and trimmed

Method:

- To bake well, an oven temperature of 400°F (200 degrees Celsius) should be set.
- Mix the olive oil, salt, & pepper with the cut Brussels sprouts.
- Roast at 400 degrees for twenty minutes in total or as long as tender if spread out in a single layer.
- Whisk together the tahini, the juice of one lemon, the garlic cloves, & water to make a dressing for your salad.
- To adjust the consistency, add water as needed.
- Serve your roasted Brussels sprouts with a drizzle of the tahini dressing.

Calories: 180-200

Nutrition: Rich in fiber, vitamins, and healthy fats.

26. Broccoli Rice Pilaf

Time required to Prepare it: 10 mins

Time required to Cook it: 15 mins

Portions: 2

Ingredients:

- 1 medium head of cauliflower (or broccoli), grated into "rice"
- 2 tbsp of slivered almonds
- 1/2 cup of peas
- Pepper and salt to adjust the taste
- 1 tbsp olive oil
- 1 tsp of turmeric powder

Method:

- In a blender, broccoli and cauliflower florets can be ground down until they have a consistency similar to rice.
- A skillet containing olive oil ought to be heated over a low to medium flame.
- For around three to four mins in a sauté pan, the shredded broccoli and cauliflower rice will soften just enough to be edible.
- Combine the ground turmeric with the peas. Increase the time by two mins.
- Put in as much Pepper and salt as you like.
- Add the sliced almonds and stir.
- Cauliflower or as broccoli rice pilaf is a tasty and healthy alternative to traditional rice pilaf.

Calories: 150-180

Nutrition: Low in sugar and other carbohydrates, high in fiber, but nutritionally dense.

27. Grilled Asparagus and Quinoa Salad

Time required to Prepare it: 10 mins

Time required to Cook it: 15 mins

Portions: 4

Ingredients:

- 1 bunch trimmed asparagus
- 1/4 cup crumbled goat cheese (or choose vegan cheese)
- 2 tbsp olive oil
- Pepper and salt as per your preference
- 1/4 cup mint
- Juice of 1 lemon
- 1 cup cooked quinoa

Method:

- The grill or grill pan should be heated at medium-high temperatures.
- Add some salt, pepper, and olive oil to the asparagus and toss.
- Cook the asparagus on the grill for about three to five mins, turning it once or twice, until it is tender and has a faint sear.
- Mix together the quinoa, grilled asparagus, fresh mint, and goat cheese (or what vegan cheese) in a dish after everything is made.
- Lemon juice and zest should be squeezed over the salad before serving.
- If more Pepper and salt are required, add them now.
- Hot or at room temperature, this grilled asparagus & quinoa salad is delicious.

Calories: 200-250

Nutrition: Provides a balance of protein, fiber, and fresh flavors.

28. Spinach and Mushroom Quinoa Stuffed Bell Peppers

Time required to Prepare it: 10 mins

Time required to Cook it: 20 mins

Portions: 2

Ingredients:

- 1 tsp of Italian seasoning
- 1 cup of chopped baby spinach
- 2 tbsp of olive oil
- 1 cup of chopped mushrooms
- 1/4 cup of diced red onion
- Pepper and salt to adjust the taste
- 2 large bell peppers
- 1 cup of cooked quinoa

- 1/4 cup of grated mozzarella cheese (or consider vegan cheese)

Method:

- It is suggested that oven temperature be set to 375 F (190 C).
- A skillet containing olive oil ought to be heated over a low to medium flame.
- Combine the red onion and mushrooms. Wait a few mins for the mushrooms to shed their liquid before serving.
- Cook the baby spinach until it wilts after being added to the pan. Salt, pepper, & Italian spice are great seasonings to use.
- Combine the cooked quinoa with the mushroom and spinach mixture in a bowl.
- Stuff the quinoa mixture into the bell pepper slices.
- Sprinkle some shredded mozzarella (or even vegan cheese) on top of the stuffed peppers.
- After around 20 mins in a preheated oven, the peppers ought to be tender & the cheese must be melted.
- Serve the spinach and mushroom quinoa stuffed bell peppers warm.

Calories: 250-300

Nutrition: Offers an ideal ratio of protein to fiber to vitamin content.

Chapter 6: Guilt-free Treats

29. Dark Chocolate and Berry Parfait

Time required to Prepare it: 10 mins

Time required to Cook it: 5 mins

Portions: 2

Ingredients:

- 1 cup Greek yogurt (or coconut yogurt for a vegan version)
- 1/4 cup of dark chocolate chunks or chips
- 1 tbsp of honey or maple syrup (optional for added sweetness)

- Fresh mint leaves for garnish (optional)
- 1 cup of mixed berries

Method:

- Greek yogurt should be used as the base layer in presenting glasses or bowls.
- Sprinkle an even coating of mixed berries over the yogurt.
- Over the berries, scatter small pieces of dark chocolate.
- Keep layering until you've run out of ingredients or the parfait has reached the desired height.
- Honey and maple syrup can be used as an optional sweetener to drizzle between the layers.
- Fresh mint leaves make a great garnish.
- The parfait can be served right away or stored in the fridge till later.

Calories: 250-300

Nutrition: Rich in protein, antioxidants, and healthy fats.

30. Nut Butter Banana Bites

Time required to Prepare it: 5 mins

Time required to Cook it: 0 mins

Portions: 2

Ingredients:

- 2 bananas, peeled and sliced
- 4 tbsp nut or seed butter
- 2 tsps chia seeds

Method:

- Lay the banana slices on a plate or serving dish.
- Using a spoon, carefully dollop a bit of nut or seed butter onto each banana slice.
- Sprinkle chia seeds over the nut butter-topped banana slices.

- Serve the nut butter banana bites immediately.

Calories: 200-250 (varies based on ingredients and portion sizes)

Nutrition: Provides healthy fats, protein, and fiber.

31. Almond Butter Energy Bites

Time required to Prepare it: 10 mins

Time to Set: 20 mins (in the refrigerator)

Portions: 12-15 bites

Ingredients:

- 1/4 cup chopped nuts
- 1/2 cup almond butter
- Some salt
- 1/4 cup ground flaxseed
- 1 tsp vanilla extract
- 1/4 cup honey or maple syrup
- 1/4 cup mini dark chocolate chips
- 1/4 cup rolled oats

Method:

- Roll the oats and add them to a big bowl along with the almond butter, honey, maple syrup, ground flaxseed, mini dark-colored chocolate chips, vanilla extract, and a pinch of salt.
- Blend thoroughly so that everything is uniformly distributed.
- If you want to work with the mixture more easily, chill it in the fridge for 30 mins.
- Once the mixture has cold, scoop out small amounts and shape them into balls.
- Spread the energy bites out on a dish or tray coated with parchment paper.
- Refrigerate the energy bites for an additional 20 mins to firm up.
- Serve the almond butter energy bites as a guilt-free treat.

Calories: 100-120

Nutrition: Packed with energy, healthy fats, and fiber.

32. Greek Yogurt Parfait with Mixed Nuts and Honey

Time required to Prepare it: 10 mins

Time required to Cook it: 0 mins

Portions: 2

Ingredients:

- 1/4 cup of chopped mixed nuts (such as walnuts, almonds, pistachios)
- 1 cup of Greek yogurt (or opt for plant-based yogurt for a vegan choice)
- 2 tbsp of honey (or use maple syrup for a vegan alternative)
- Fresh berries or sliced fruits for topping

Method:

- Greek yogurt, minced mixed nuts, and honey (or what maple syrup) are delicious served in individual glasses or bowls.
- You can add as many levels as you like.
- Add your favorite sliced fruits or fresh berries on top.
- Serve the Greek yogurt parfait immediately.

Calories: 250-300

Nutrition: Rich in protein, healthy fats, and natural sweetness.

33. Chocolate Dipped Strawberries

Time required to Prepare it: 15 mins

Time to Set: 15 mins (in the refrigerator)

Portions: Varies

Ingredients:

- Fresh strawberries, washed and dried
- Dark chocolate or semi-sweet chocolate chips (70% cocoa or higher)

Optional toppings: chopped nuts, shredded coconut, chia seeds

Method:

- Cover a baking surface or as a serving plate with parchment paper.

- Heat the chocolate chips in the microwave, stirring after each interval of 20 seconds, until smooth.
- Dip a strawberry in the melted chocolate, holding it by the stem so the extra chocolate may drip off.
- You can sprinkle the chocolate-covered strawberry with nuts, coconut, and chia seeds if you choose.
- Set the coated strawberry on the plate or tray you've previously prepared.
- The remaining strawberries should be treated in the same manner.
- If you want to set the chocolate on the dipped strawberries, put them in the fridge for about 15 mins.
- The chocolate-covered strawberries will make a delicious dessert.

Calories: 40-50

Nutrition: Offers a touch of indulgence with antioxidants and natural sweetness.

Conclusion

In closing, this cookbook has been a culinary journey aimed at delivering quick, wholesome, and delicious meals that perfectly align with your busy lifestyle. Throughout this cookbook, we've explored a diverse array of breakfasts, starters, speedy suppers, smart sides, and guilt-free treats, all curated to help you achieve your health and wellness goals without sacrificing taste or precious time.

As we conclude, it's crucial to reiterate the significance of incorporating clean proteins and fresh vegetables into our daily meals. These nutrient-rich components are the backbone of a balanced diet, providing essential building blocks for our bodies and empowering us to lead vibrant lives.

In our pursuit of health-conscious eating, we've provided you with a range of recipes that serve as a canvas for your culinary creativity. Feel free to experiment with your own healthy twists, swapping ingredients to suit your preferences and dietary needs. The kitchen is a realm of endless possibilities, and these recipes are merely stepping stones toward your own unique culinary adventure.

In the midst of our busy lives, it's easy to overlook the importance of nourishing ourselves adequately. However, this cookbook serves as a reminder that nourishment need not be compromised during hectic times. By embracing the recipes within these pages, you're equipping yourself with the tools to maintain a wholesome diet, even on the busiest of days.

Thank you for embarking on this culinary journey with me. Here's to a future filled with nutritious, satisfying and expedient meals that support your well-being, nourish your body and inspire a lifelong commitment to healthy eating. Remember, every meal is an opportunity to prioritise your health and savour the goodness that comes from wholesome ingredients. Happy cooking and bon appétit!

Yours In Health,

Dr Kris Harm

Printed in Great Britain
by Amazon